Is hell for real?

And other questions about judgment, eternity and the God of love

Erik Raymond

thegoodbook
COMPANY

Questions
Christians ask

Is hell for real?
And other questions about judgment, eternity and the God of love
Part of the *Questions Christians Ask* series
© Erik Raymond/The Good Book Company, 2017

Published by
The Good Book Company
Tel (UK): 0333 123 0880
Tel (North America): (1) 866 244 2165
International: +44 (0) 208 942 0880
Email (UK): info@thegoodbook.co.uk
Email (North America): info@thegoodbook.com

Websites
UK & Europe: www.thegoodbook.co.uk
North America: www.thegoodbook.com
Australia: www.thegoodbook.com.au
New Zealand: www.thegoodbook.co.nz

ISBN: 9781784980689 | Printed in the UK

Design by André Parker

Contents

Introduction:
A day at the Falls...   **5**

1. Is hell real?   **15**

2. What is hell like?   **29**

3. The reason for hell   **37**

4. Please... don't go to hell   **57**

Appendix 1:
Alternative views on hell   **73**

Appendix 2:
Frequently asked questions about hell   **81**

Acknowledgements   **95**

*"I am the Living One; I was dead, and now look,
I am alive for ever and ever! And I hold the keys
of death and Hades."*

Revelation 1 v 18

A day at the Falls…

This past summer as my family was driving through upstate New York, we decided to stop at Niagara Falls. The view is simply breathtaking.

From the rail above the Niagara River you can see three giant waterfalls. The volume of water that flows over the Falls is difficult to take in. In a minute there are 600,000 gallons of water flowing over the waterfalls on the Canadian side and 150,000 gallons on the American. The air is filled with spray. The roar and noise is deafening. You try to imagine how many gallons of water have flowed over these Falls in the last hundred years. It is truly beyond comprehension.

But as I stood there overlooking the waterfall, my mind was drawn in a different direction. Instead of thinking about the astounding beauty of nature, I began thinking about the horror of hell. Humanity is like a river that starts small, and grows as it threads its way through life. But, like the Niagara river, at the end, there is only one place to go. Over the Falls.

I began to compute. Last year over 55 million people

died in the world. That's over 150,000 a day, 6,300 a hour, 105 a minute. Nearly two people every second breathe their last in this world. How many of them are not Christians? If we take a very generous estimate and say that half of them are believers in Jesus, then that would mean, according to traditional Christian teaching, that about 75,000 people each day find themselves facing an eternity not in heaven, but in "the other place".

Asking the right questions

There I stood, looking at the unceasing torrent pouring into the boiling chaos below, and my heart was shredded. I thought about the sheer volume of people that die, passing over the threshold of life and ending up, if Christian teaching is correct, in hell. And I admit to you that I struggled with it. My struggle was rational and humanitarian before it was biblical.

Rational, because it just doesn't seem to make sense. I looked around at the happy crowds eating ice cream and having fun. What could they have done to deserve such a fate? How could it be that so many would have to endure such an eternity?

Humanitarian, because, why would God create such wonderful, warm, gifted and delightful human beings, only to throw them away on the scrap heap of eternity?

And once the questions started, they didn't stop. How could this many people go to hell every single day? But more deeply, I asked myself, "How is it possible that God could be honored by this?" I know that God is good, loving, and merciful. I believe this with everything that I am—unwaveringly so. But as the mist from the Falls landed on my arm and I leaned on the railing, I couldn't help but struggle through the questions. "How does this serve to show God's goodness, love and mercy?"

Have you ever struggled with questions like these? I'm sure you have. Believe me, you're not alone. Along with many others who have thought carefully and seriously about the Bible's teaching on hell, you've most certainly asked some hard questions. That moment of bewilderment at Niagara was not the first time I've thought this through. And I don't think it will be the last. The idea of hell, as it is presented to us in the Bible, confronts us with a sobering disruption. Like a noisy alarm being set off within our souls, when the subject is raised, our minds begin racing and our hearts are gripped. The gravity of the matter won't allow us to simply put it aside.

Is it true that the Bible teaches that those who reject Christ will spend eternity enduring the conscious torment of hell as a judgment upon their sin? These are questions we would rather avoid, but as feeling human beings, it is important that we face them.

And let me make it absolutely clear: *these are also good and appropriate questions to ask.* Wind back the clock twenty years to when I was not yet a Christian and talk to me about hell, and I likely would have laughed in your face. We shouldn't be surprised when people are hostile to the big ideas of the gospel—either angry or mocking. If they are open to listening and thinking, they will need to work through their concerns about the gospel message, and this will take time, patience, and honesty. Questions about hell are not off-limits. As Christians we are to be equipped both to know and provide a reasonable explanation of God's word:

> Always be prepared to give an answer to everyone who asks you to give the reason for the hope that you have. But do this with gentleness and respect.
>
> *1 Peter 3 v 15*

Peter imagines a situation where someone asks you: "Why do you think you will go to heaven when you die?" He is keen that we do not sit there silent or spluttering and incomprehensible. So, before we can give a reasonable defense of our hope to others, we must be able to answer the questions we are asking. Questions about what will happen when we die, about the judgment we face, and about the existence and nature of hell are key questions that must be answered. And behind all these questions are the bigger "bedrock" questions about God's character. How can he be a God of love, and yet judge? How can he be kind and forgiving, and yet speak about an eternity of hell-fire?

The right resource

I mentioned that my questions were rational and humanitarian before they were biblical. This does not mean my questions were invalid, but they were just incomplete. Because before we begin to answer these questions, we must see what the Bible actually says. I suspect that many of us have a view of judgment and hell that is more informed by medieval paintings, jokey cartoon depictions, or half-remembered terrifying sermons from fire-brand preachers, than by Scripture. The Bible, after all, is our only reliable source of knowledge about God, and the way he reveals truth to people.

Several years ago, popular speaker, author, and pastor Rob Bell ignited a massive controversy within the Christian world with his book *Love Wins*. The book begins by asking many of the same types of questions that I ask in this introduction. Buckling under the sobering weight of humanitarian and rational objections, Bell offers another solution. He favors a position similar to what has historically been called "universalism"—that, in the end, *everyone* will be saved. Hell will be empty. In this book we will arrive at a different conclusion. But this is not because I have forsaken humanitarian or rational concerns. Quite the contrary. When we read the Bible, we find that most of the teaching about hell comes from the mouth of Jesus—the most loving and compassionate and wisest man who ever lived.

As Christians, our primary authoritative source for answers to questions like these *must* be the Bible in general, and the teaching of Jesus in particular. As human beings we are finite; we have limited knowledge and experience. Therefore, not knowing about hell by experience (thankfully) or through exhaustive knowledge, we require a source that has the knowledge. For centuries Christians have turned to the Scriptures for such answers. We do this because we believe that in the Scriptures, God has provided everything we need to know in order to faithfully follow him. This doctrine, known as "the sufficiency of Scripture," teaches that we have what we need in order to answer the questions we need answers to. And as we will see, the subject of hell is not something that God has been cryptic or unclear about. He has laid out this matter with repetition and clarity. This encourages us both to study and to confidently rest in what God's word says, rather than adding to it, subtracting from it, or completely ignoring it.

I do not fault Bell and others for their questions—I ask them too. However, I do take issue with how the questions are answered. When we dial down the teaching of Scripture, because it does not fit our culture or feelings, or when it seems to make no sense, then we cease to think as Christians.

The right tone

The consideration of hell will make demands on our willingness to be faithful to God and his word. But we must be faithful not only in matters of doctrine but also to the corresponding tone with which the Bible explains and communicates these truths.

You may well have, regrettably, encountered a degree of flippancy regarding the subject of hell. On the one hand, there are those who do not regard the Bible as God's word. They reject the concept of hell as ridiculous and laughable, and consider those who believe in it to be ignorant and outdated. It is laughed off with jokes and sneers, like the line that came back at me when I was pleading with an unbelieving friend: "Why wouldn't I want to go to hell? All my friends will be there."

At the other extreme, there are professing Christians who, sadly, seem to *enjoy* pronouncing words of condemnation and eternal ruin upon those who are outside the faith. With some sort of warped sense of joy, they treat with contempt those who are heading to eternal darkness. It makes me cringe. I hope it does the same to you.

By contrast, there is an appropriate way to speak about this. Upon learning that his friend had preached on hell the previous day, one pastor asked, "Did you preach it with tears?" This seems like a fitting question to calibrate our hearts. If we approach this subject with seriousness, and tears in our eyes, then we are following our Lord. He knew that God's judgment would soon fall on Jerusalem, because the people of the city had rejected him. Was his reaction indifference? *No.* Did he rejoice that they were getting their just desserts? *No.*

> As he approached Jerusalem and saw the city, he wept over it and said, "If you, even you, had only known on this day what would bring you peace – but now it is hidden from your eyes."
>
> *Luke 19 v 41-42*

Those who seek to follow Jesus should emulate both his compassion for others and his concern for the glory of God.

Answering the questions

Let's face it: hell is a topic that most of us don't feel very comfortable talking (or reading) about. Thinking about eternal suffering is unsettling—and rightly so. I believe this to be deliberate on God's part. But this does not mean that we shouldn't talk about it. Consider the work of a cancer doctor who spends significant years researching, writing, and discussing what she can know about the disease. Why does she do this? Because she cares about people—and because cancer is a real, serious threat to life. To neglect her study is to neglect the very purpose of her job—to care for others.

So as we consider hell together—both its certainty and severity—who would object to intentionally setting aside a little time to consider how to better understand it and help people avoid it?

As I have been researching and reading about this uncomfortable subject, I've spoken with many different people about it—both Christian and not. It's been interesting to hear their fears, struggles, and questions. One friend who has been a Christian for several decades shared how this teaching causes him more unrest than anything else in the Bible. A woman with young children told me how difficult she finds it to explain to her kids. An older saint who is, humanly speaking, closer to death than many, talked about his persistent doubts on the subject.

Another friend who is a relatively new Christian shared how his understanding of hell had led to a deep concern for his unbelieving family and friends. In his conversations with them, he is drawn to talking openly and asking questions about the exclusivity of Christ and the reality of hell. In a talk with a non-Christian friend, he wanted to get right down to business, as he said, about what the Bible actually teaches about hell. In my admittedly small sample, I've observed a trend of both curiosity and concern about hell. We will all benefit from taking the time to look our questions in the eye, and give ourselves an opportunity for further review and discussion.

Where are we going?

My goal in writing is not to provide an exhaustive treatment on what the Bible says about judgment, hell, and life beyond the grave. Instead, I want to provide you with an accessible and serviceable overview of the Bible's teaching on this subject. I want you to understand better what the Bible says about these weighty and important issues, and to be more equipped to answer questions.

But also, if you are a Christian, I hope to grow a sense of worshipful gratitude in you through a greater understanding of what the Lord endured to rescue you from hell. We are asking and answering the most common big question, "Is hell for real?", but in each chapter we will ask and answer several underlying questions.

- In chapter one we'll consider whether hell is a real place, or simply just a picture or metaphor for something else.

- In chapter two we explore what hell is like according to Jesus and the other Bible writers.

- In chapter three we will think through the reason for hell: "Is hell really necessary?"

- Then, we will see how the main theme of the Bible's teaching is focussed—not on hell itself, but on how to *avoid* hell.

At the end, I've tried to answer objections and frequently asked questions about this most difficult of doctrines.

Amid the deafening noise of the waterfalls, my heart and mind simmered with questions. Would you join me at the observation deck? Let's bring our questions, concerns and worries to the only place where they will find a resolution.

Chapter 1

Is hell real?

I had been anticipating the conversation since meeting Dan at the gym several weeks before. We exchanged emails and scheduled a time to get together and talk about God. Dan was eager to begin reading the Bible with me and to investigate its teachings. About halfway through lunch he leaned forward and said, "So let me get this straight: *you believe there really is a hell?*"

I had mentioned in passing something about how we needed to have faith in Christ, and how Jesus was the only way, and Dan pounced on it.

I gave him a profound theological answer that was sound, biblical and concise.

I simply said, *"Yes."*

But while the answer was true and admirably brief—it was not sufficient. A question this big requires some careful and faithful nuancing. There needed to be some spadework done, some dirt turned over, before a flag could be squarely planted in the answer.

Before I go into how I would answer this, let me ask

you a question. How would you answer Dan? Where would you begin?

As we have already seen, any conversation about hell requires biblical fidelity in both truth and tone. We need to have the right content communicated with appropriate concern.

So, let's get to work.

A growing understanding

As we turn to Scripture for our answer, we must remember that the Bible, while it is a unified book with tremendous continuity, is also a collection of many smaller books written by over forty authors spanning over 1,500 years. And like any good story, the Bible develops its concepts, themes, and plot over time. Theologians refer to this as "progressive revelation." Simply put, this means that God reveals more details about particular subjects as the Bible progresses. God doesn't tell us everything we need to know in the early chapters of Genesis. What God may have revealed in seed form early on comes into full bloom in the later books, particularly with the coming of our Lord Jesus Christ. A familiar example of this is in the Christmas story, where the angels announce to the shepherds:

> "Today in the town of David a Savior has been born to you; he is the Messiah, the Lord."
>
> *Luke 2 v 11*

At long last, the promised son of David has come and is in the city of David (Micah 5 v 2). But this announcement only has such tremendous weight because it has been so extensively "trailed" throughout the Bible story. The promise of a Savior sent by God has been fermenting since Genesis chapter 3 when Adam and Eve first sinned (Genesis 3 v 15). God had promised a son from the line of Eve who would crush Satan and as a result bring relief from the curse that was feared and felt on that fateful day.

This broad promise of a Savior would narrow throughout the Bible as God progressively revealed more and more details about his promised King. So, in addition to learning that it is Eve's offspring who will crush the serpent's head, we discover that he will also come from Abraham (Genesis 12 v 1-3), Isaac (22 v 15-18), Jacob (28 v 13-15), Judah (Genesis 49 v 9-10), and David (2 Samuel 7 v 12-16), and that he will be born in the city of David or Bethlehem (Micah 5 v 2). The tiny acorn of an idea in Genesis grows slowly into the budding oak tree in Luke chapter 2.

And on the subject of hell, we see the same slow revelation over time. Surveying the entire Bible, we see progressive revelation at play, shaping and informing our understanding of hell.

Old Testament teaching

The Old Testament writers use the Hebrew word *Sheol* to describe the grave or the place of the dead (e.g. Genesis 37 v 35; Job 17 v 13-16; Psalm 6 v 5; 16 v 10; Isaiah 14 v 11). This dark and shady place has little detail attached to it; it seems at first, that this is simply a catch-all description of "the place where dead people go." But careful readers will notice the concept of some kind of separation between those who are "unrighteous" or "wicked" and "the assembly of the righteous"—those who belong to God's people, as they instead are experiencing God's judgment.

> But if the Lord creates something new, and the ground opens its mouth and swallows them up with all that belongs to them, and they go down alive into Sheol, then you shall know that these men have despised the Lord." And as soon as he had finished speaking all these words, the ground under them split apart. And the earth opened its mouth and swallowed them up, with their households and all the people who belonged to Korah and all their goods. So they and all that belonged to them went down alive into Sheol, and the earth closed over them, and they perished from the midst of the assembly. And all Israel who were around them fled at their cry, for they said, "Lest the earth swallow us up!" And fire came out from the Lord and consumed the 250 men offering the incense." *Numbers 16 v 30-35 (ESV)*

> The wicked shall return to Sheol, all the nations that forget God. *Psalm 9 v 17 (ESV)*

> Let death steal over them; let them go down to Sheol alive; for evil is in their dwelling place and in their heart. *Psalm 55 v 15 (ESV)*

For Sheol does not thank you; death does not praise you; those who go down to the pit do not hope for your faithfulness. *Isaiah 38 v 18* (ESV)

For as the new heavens and the new earth that I make shall remain before me, says the Lord, so shall your offspring and your name remain. From new moon to new moon, and from Sabbath to Sabbath, all flesh shall come to worship before me, declares the Lord. And they shall go out and look on the dead bodies of the men who have rebelled against me. For their worm shall not die, their fire shall not be quenched, and they shall be an abhorrence to all flesh. *Isaiah 66 v 22-24* (ESV)

At that time shall arise Michael, the great prince who has charge of your people. And there shall be a time of trouble, such as never has been since there was a nation till that time. But at that time your people shall be delivered, everyone whose name shall be found written in the book. And many of those who sleep in the dust of the earth shall awake, some to everlasting life, and some to shame and everlasting contempt. *Daniel 12 v 1–2*

While not as developed as the bigger picture we discover in the New Testament, nevertheless, the concept of hell is there, and bears a striking similarity to the developed teaching of punishment, banishment, and destruction later in the Bible.

New Testament teaching

By the time we reach the New Testament, however, a lot more detail has been filled in. There are three main Greek words that refer to the place of judgment, and are often translated as "hell" in our Bibles: *Hades*, *Tartarus*, and *Gehenna*.

Hades

Hades, is most often used the way *Sheol* is used in the Old Testament to refer to the grave—the place where the dead go (Luke 10 v 15; 16 v 23; Acts 2 v 27; Revelation 1 v 18, 20 v 13-14). *Hades* had a history in Greek mythology. He was the "god" of the underworld, where dead souls go, and his realm became known by his name. When searching for a way to express the truths in the Old Testament (OT) about life beyond the grave, the translators of the OT into Greek chose the word *Hades*. This doesn't mean they agreed with Greek mythology and its "gods"—just that it was a word that people knew and associated with the afterlife and underworld.

Tartarus

Tartarus is a rare word, used only in 2 Peter 2 v 4, where it is translated as "sent … to hell." It refers to a literal place where its occupants (here fallen angels) are in chains and darkness while awaiting the final judgment. Again, *Tartarus* has its origins in Greek mythology. It was the part of *Hades* where the worst people were thrown—a deep abyss that was used as a dungeon of torment and suffering for the wicked. The Bible writers used these familiar words to represent a similar yet fundamentally different idea of what happens at death. They clothed their teaching about God's just judgement in this familiar language as they reached out with the gospel to the Greek-speaking world.

Gehenna

Finally, there is the word *Gehenna*. This is by far the most common word in the New Testament, occurring twelve times, with the overwhelming majority of references coming from the teaching of Jesus. It is a word that had contemporary significance and provided a reference point to explain the coming judgment.

Gehenna, was a place in the valley of Hinnom on the south side of Jerusalem, where all rubbish from the city would be dumped and burned. The fire here was always burning. Perhaps as Jesus was teaching in the temple or elsewhere, he could point to the plume of black smoke rising in the distance. It is a powerful picture of rubbish that is thrown away and is being consumed by fire. The Lord Jesus uses this image to refer to a literal place of final punishment for those who reject God's word.

It is important to note that most of what Christians believe about hell comes from the mouth of Jesus. Many people contrast the teachings of Jesus with the teachings of the Old Testament. It's common to hear people speak of their preference for Jesus because he is "so much more loving" than the God of the Old Testament.

This perception about the Bible is simply not true.

There are wonderful promises of grace throughout the Old Testament Scriptures, like this one:

The LORD, the LORD, the compassionate and gracious God, slow to anger, abounding in love and faithfulness, maintaining love to thousands, and forgiving wickedness, rebellion and sin.

Exodus 34:6-7

And there are repeated and serious warnings of God's wrath in the New. If we study Jesus's teaching with an eye toward this topic we will find that he seems to be quite at home speaking about hell. It has been correctly observed that Jesus talked more about hell than heaven. Evidently he believed in the existence of hell and wanted others to also. In other words, the doctrine of hell was not only a settled matter for the Lord Jesus, but he also considered it vitally important for his hearers to understand. His warnings are uncompromising:

"But I tell you that anyone who is angry with a brother or sister will be subject to judgment. Again, anyone who says to a brother or sister, 'Raca,' is answerable to the court. And anyone who says, 'You fool!' will be in danger of the fire of hell.
Matthew 5 v 22

He advocated people taking extreme measures to ensure that they don't go to hell:

"It is better for you to lose one part of your body than for your whole body to be thrown into hell."
Matthew 5 v 29

He cautioned against misplaced fear by urging people not to fear man who can simply kill the body but,

> "Fear him who, after your body has been killed, has authority to throw you into hell. Yes, I tell you, fear him."   *Luke 12 v 5*

Among people who spoke as freely as we do today, he instructed them of the coming day of judgment when

> "But I tell you that everyone will have to give account on the day of judgment for every empty word they have spoken."   *Matthew 12 v 36*

He portrayed the day of judgment as a time when a king will sit on his glorious throne to separate people based upon their deeds. The consequence for disregard of the king and his words is penetrating:

> "Depart from me, you who are cursed, into the eternal fire prepared for the devil and his angels."   *Matthew 25 v 41*

Jesus took the title of judge and applied it to himself, saying that he has "authority to judge" (John 5 v 27).

Jesus also believed and taught that there will be a physical bodily resurrection of all people:

> "Do not be amazed at this, for a time is coming when all who are in their graves will hear his voice and come out—those who have done what is good will rise to live, and those who have done

what is evil will rise to be condemned."

John 5 v 28-29

Notice that Jesus is saying that *everyone* will be raised to life at the last day. At this point there will be a distinction made between those who have done good and those who have done evil. Those who have done good are simply those who have received the message of the gospel, putting their faith in Christ and repenting of their sins. The evil, on the other hand, are those who have died in their sins, rejecting God's rule over them. Those who are forgiven inherit eternal life, and those who remain unforgiven inherit eternal judgment.

I take it that the Lord Jesus spoke so openly, plainly and clearly about hell is that he knew it to be real, and that he didn't want *anyone* to go there. In fact, it is the very reason he was came—so that no one *need* go there.

The history of hell

Throughout the history of the church this view—death, then resurrection, then judgment, then division based on faith in Christ—has been the dominant belief held by Christians. It wasn't until the modern period that this understanding of Jesus' teaching began to be questioned. The main strands of disagreement came in three forms:

- **Universalism** believes that in the end all people will ultimately be saved—regardless of any lack of repentance and trust in Christ.

- **Conditional immortality** maintains that only

Christians receive the gift of immortality, while non-Christians do not (and as a result their existence ends upon their death).

- **Annihilationism** suggests that those who are not Christians will experience a season of suffering after death, but after a time they will be annihilated.

We will interact with each of these ideas a bit later in this book,[1] but for now, it is important to note that Jesus does not simply speak about heaven in eternal terms but also about judgment in hell.

> "Then they will go away to eternal punishment,
> but the righteous to eternal life."
>
> *Matthew 25 v 46*

If we were to summarize and synthesize Christ's teaching on the subject of hell, it would be straightforward and consistent with the rest of the Bible writers. The graphic pictures and language he used to describe it, show that Jesus believed hell to be a place of punishment, destruction and banishment. One writer sums it up like this:

Punishment is frequently portrayed as retribution, judgment, suffering and torment by fire. Destruction is often described as perishing, death, or the second death. Banishment is commonly pictured

---

1 See Appendix 1: Alternative views on hell

as separation from the kingdom of God, exclusion from the presence of God, or being cut off from something living."[2]

Our instinct to draw away from what seems to us a harsh and uncompromising doctrine creates a problem. It is inconsistent for us to drop the clear biblical teaching about judgment and hell while maintaining its complementary teaching about forgiveness and heaven.

Many have wondered if they can dial down the severity of hell by adopting a Conditional Immortality, or Annihilationist viewpoint, but these views are hard to sustain from a plain reading of Scripture. It is clear that all people will be raised on the last day. We know that everyone will face judgment (Hebrews 9 v 27). And we know that the judgement day will be a horrific experience for those who have rejected Christ. *But what then?*

In Jesus' story of the sheep and the goats, the same Greek word is used in both instances; the punishment of the wicked and the blessing of the righteous are both *eternal* (Matthew 25 v 46). The two are correlated. While I understand and empathize with those who are unsettled by this doctrine, I cannot find relief from the gruesome reality of hell by manipulating the clear teaching of Jesus. A true love for others is founded upon a love for God and his word; it cannot come at the expense of these.

---

2   Christopher W. Morgan, and Robert A. Peterson, *Hell under fire: modern scholarship reinvents eternal punishment* (Zondervan, 2004).

Letting God answer our questions

Returning to the conversation with my friend Dan, what was clear is that he wanted straightforward, biblically-supported answers. While my initial answer may have surprised him a bit, he was also intrigued. He wanted to know more. He wanted to know what Christians believe and why. He was on a quest for truth. If you are not yet a follower of Jesus, don't be put off by answers that you may not agree with initially. Instead of dismissing them out of hand, investigate them more fully. Look at the original sources and study what they teach. Do your best to understand what the Bible says. I can assure you that this will not be a waste of your time.

On the other hand, if you are already a Christian, the Bible teaches that you need to be able to give a reasonable answer for what you believe and why you believe it (1 Peter 3 v 15). The mission of seeking truth does not end when you become a follower of Jesus. Instead, it has really begun in earnest. As disciples of Jesus, we continue to pursue biblical truth in such a way that we grow in knowledge and understanding of it (2 Peter 3 v 18). We do this out of love for God and others.

Whether you are seeking answers as someone who is still investigating the Christian faith or you are someone who is a Christian, this is a worthy mission to undertake. The Bible is a trustworthy guide. As we work our way forward, I pray that God would give you understanding and wisdom as you think through this important yet sobering doctrine.

Chapter 2

What is hell like?

As we consider what the Bible says about the nature of hell, I'm sure a number of "why?" questions will begin percolating in your mind. As difficult as it may be to do, I have to ask you to hold on to those questions until we get to the next chapter—I find it helps to write them down so I don't forget. This chapter will simply deal with the "what?" question, while the next chapter will grapple with the "why?" question.

We may summarize the Bible's teaching on hell as the literal place where God administers eternal, conscious punishment for those who have sinned against him. Let's unpack that sentence phrase by phrase.

How long will hell last?

In light of the terrifying descriptions of hell, it follows that an important question to answer is its duration. *How long will it last?*

The Bible teaches that hell will last forever. In other words, it will go on eternally. Consider this sampling of verses:

[Jesus said...] "Woe to the world because of the things that cause people to stumble! Such things must come, but woe to the person through whom they come! If your hand or your foot causes you to stumble, cut it off and throw it away. It is better for you to enter life maimed or crippled than to have two hands or two feet and be thrown into eternal fire. And if your eye causes you to stumble, gouge it out and throw it away. It is better for you to enter life with one eye than to have two eyes and be thrown into the fire of hell."

Matthew 18:7-9

Jesus urges us to weigh up the benefit of living this temporal life with some degree of personal difficulty, against suffering the consequences of eternal hell. The central contrast is between temporal discomfort and eternal punishment. As others have observed, one day in hell will be far worse than a lifetime of personal sacrifice.

In an important passage at the end of Matthew's Gospel, Jesus draws the parallel between eternal life and eternal hell. The duration of both heaven and hell correspond.

When the Son of Man comes in his glory, and all the angels with him, he will sit on his glorious throne. All the nations will be gathered before him, and he will separate the people one from another as a shepherd separates the sheep from the goats. He will put the sheep on his right and the goats on his left. Then the King will say to those on his right, "Come, you who are blessed by my Father; take your inheritance, the kingdom prepared for you since the creation of the world." . . . Then he will say to those on his left, "Depart from me, you who are cursed, into the eternal fire prepared for the devil and his angels" . . . . Then they will go away to eternal punishment, but the righteous to eternal life.   *Matthew 25 v 31-46*

This is similar to what the prophet Daniel wrote.

At that time Michael, the great prince who protects your people, will arise. There will be a time of distress such as has not happened from the beginning of nations until then. But at that time your people—everyone whose name is found written in the book—will be delivered. Multitudes who sleep in the dust of the earth will awake: some to everlasting life, others to shame and everlasting contempt.   *Daniel 12 v 1-2*

The letter of Jude in the New Testament speaks of a darkness that will last forever.

They are wild waves of the sea, foaming up their shame; wandering stars, for whom blackest darkness has been reserved forever.   *Jude 13*

In the book of Revelation we read of smoke rising forever and ever with torment likewise lasting eternally.

> A third angel followed them and said in a loud voice: "If anyone worships the beast and its image and receives its mark on their forehead or on their hand, they, too, will drink the wine of God's fury, which has been poured full strength into the cup of his wrath. They will be tormented with burning sulfur in the presence of the holy angels and of the Lamb. And the smoke of their torment will rise for ever and ever. There will be no rest day or night for those who worship the beast and its image, or for anyone who receives the mark of its name."
>
> *Revelation 14 v 9-11*

It is important to note here that the judgment received by unbelievers in hell corresponds with the eternal judgment upon the beast, the false prophet, and the devil.

> And the devil, who deceived them, was thrown into the lake of burning sulfur, where the beast and the false prophet had been thrown. They will be tormented day and night for ever and ever.
>
> *Revelation 20 v 10*

When we come to the Bible inquiring as to the long hell lasts, we are met with an overwhelming answer: *hell lasts forever*. It is eternal.

The experience of hell

On occasion people experience such severe pain that they actually pass out. It's actually a result of God's common grace helping us to deal with pain. In his design, our nervous systems regulate our blood pressure. The intense pain brings a drop in blood pressure and a corresponding decrease in blood flow to the brain. God has given us a physical "cut-off system" that provides relief for our bodies and minds when we experience intense physical pain.

As we think about hell and the fact that it lasts forever, we are confronted with this sobering truth: the reality of hell involves more pain than we can possibly imagine. In our earthly lives, even those with the highest pain threshold will eventually pass out from physical pain. However, in hell, regardless of our present pain tolerance, all who suffer will suffer without a moment of reprieve from the torment. Truly this is sobering to consider.

Smoke gets in your eyes

Years ago I was working with some college students. At one of our events, we built a massive fire by a lake. As we were gathering around the fire for Bible study and discussion, a few guys went to get some more wood to keep the blaze going. They unwittingly chose a pile of wet logs that they threw on. The result, as you might imagine, was uncomfortable levels of smoke. With a shift of the wind, our evening around the fire turned into a disaster. Along with others, I got up choking and spluttering, with eyes burning, and did all I could to get away. What had started as a lovely evening turned into a coughing catastrophe. The smoke had dominated our senses.

When the Bible writers (especially the Lord Jesus) talk about hell, they use extremely vivid descriptions to portray its agonies. The reformer John Calvin suggested that it seemed as if God used these expressions "to confound all of our senses with dread." In other words, God's intention for using such strikingly intense language is to lay hold of our senses. In the Scriptures, God is communicating in such a way that he aims to dominate our senses. Like a smoky campfire, we cannot remain unaffected. Jesus, lovingly, wants the smoke to get in our eyes.

In light of this, consider again the vivid imagery associated with hell in the Scriptures.

In hell there is:

- weeping and gnashing of teeth (Matthew 8 v 12; 22 v 13).
- fiery furnaces (Matthew 13 v 42, 50)
- unquenchable fire (Matthew 3 v 12; Mark 9 v 43; Isaiah 66 v 24)
- outer darkness (Matthew 22 v 13).

In a parable depicting the suffering of the unrighteous upon their death, Jesus told a story of a man who was rich in this life but suffered in eternity. It is worth reading in full and reflecting on:

There was a rich man who was dressed in purple and fine linen and lived in luxury every day. At his gate was laid a beggar named Lazarus, covered with sores and longing to eat what fell from the rich man's table. Even the dogs came and licked his sores. The time came when the beggar died and the angels carried him to Abraham's side. The rich man also died and was buried. In Hades, where he was in torment, he looked up and saw Abraham far away, with Lazarus by his side. So he called to him, "Father Abraham, have pity on me and send Lazarus to dip the tip of his finger in water and cool my tongue, because I am in agony in this fire." But Abraham replied, "Son, remember that in your lifetime you received your good things, while Lazarus received bad things, but now he is comforted here and you are in agony. And besides all this, between us and you a great chasm has been set in place, so that those who want to go from here to you cannot, nor can anyone cross over from there to us."   *Luke 16 v 19-26*

The man cries for mercy and pleads for someone to be sent to dip the end of their finger "in water and cool my tongue, because I am in agony in this fire." But there is no possibility of relief. The language employed here is so descriptive one can almost feel the pain from the gnashing teeth, smell the burning fire, see the licking flames, and hear the agonizing cries for relief. The descriptions of hell from the divine pen are arresting.

And it underlines the self torture experienced those in hell: anguish at their rejection of God; regret for a wasted life; and seeing the glory and wonder of heaven that they can never take part in. They were made for loving relationship with God and others, but must endure mere existence without either.

As I read these words from Jesus and write these words of summary and explanation, I am affected—distraught even. This is truly terrible. To be honest, my natural reflex is to walk away from it or, at the very least, soften it. It is *so* terrible that I want to make it seem less awful, less bad.

But, as we have seen, this is what our loving Lord Jesus, and the whole of the Bible, teaches. Therefore, as unsettling as it may be, we must embrace it as the truth. For us to "declaw" the Bible of its thunderous judgments is not good, but evil. And to soften Scripture's sharp edges concerning hell is neither humble nor loving. In the end it is prideful because it asserts that I know better than God. And it is unloving because it veils the truth from others while changing the very word of God.

It is not wrong to feel distressed or even repulsed, and to ask our difficult questions, but we must be sure that we go to the Bible for the answers, and in doing so let God say *his* piece on *his* terms. Remember, God's ways are not our ways (Isaiah 55 v 8). He retains a reason for it. The imagery used to describe hell is intentionally intrusive; it means to arrest our senses and, ultimately, draw our souls to bow before God's word.

Who's in charge?

To this point I have not discussed a vital question: who is in charge of hell? We have considered the existence of hell and what the Bible says about its nature, but we have not given consideration to whose idea this was. And if hell is the result of a mastermind, then why? Let's dig in and consider this in the next chapter.

Chapter 3

The reason for hell

"**W**ell, I don't think a good God would ever send people there."

As I talked with my barber about the Bible, he articulated a view held by many today. I appreciated his honesty and candor—and his self-control as he held the scissors inches from my ear. As I probed further, his reasoning became clear: he did not believe that people deserved such a sentence, and he did not believe that a good God would ever do such a thing. In other words, his issue had to do with what we as people deserve, and who God is.

It's important for us to remember these points of tension in my barber's question; I believe it is at the heart of the issue for many on this subject. The Bible (and most Christians throughout church history) believe that it is God who created hell, sends people there in judgment, and will forever oversee it enduring throughout eternity.

That's a lot to take in.

Here in this chapter we will try to work out why hell is necessary. To do that we have to start with a biblical understanding of who God is and why he would ever send anyone there in judgment.

Who is God?

Early on in the Bible, when God's people lived under slavery in Egypt, God met with Moses. He sent him to speak to Pharaoh and to lead the children of Israel out of captivity (Exodus 3). This scene, famously known as the "burning bush," conveys some of the difficulty we have in answering the question: who is God? Moses asks how he should explain to the people of Israel who God is. God says that he should tell them he is the God of Abraham, Isaac and Jacob, and then cryptically adds

> God said to Moses, "I AM WHO I AM. This is what you are to say to the Israelites: 'I AM has sent me to you.'"   *Exodus 3 v 14*

"I am who I am" is the meaning of God's name *Yahweh*. It can also be translated as "I will be what I will be." The point is that God will not just *say* who he is, but *reveal* who he is through what he does and how he relates to his people. We have seen how there is a progressive revelation of the realities of hell through the Bible story. In the same way, there is a progressive revelation of the *character* and *purposes* of God through the Bible story— through his dealings with his people Israel. The Bible is the record of that revelation, which reaches its climax with the coming of Jesus—who is "the image of the invisible God" (Colossians 1 v 15).

Like Moses before us, we are in need of revelation, and we find it in the Scriptures, and especially in the life and teaching of Jesus.

God's character

- **God is eternal:** To say that God is eternal means that he has no beginning and no end. There was never a time that God did not exist, nor will there ever be such a time (Psalm 90 v 2).

- **God is infinite:** God is both omnipresent and omnipotent. In other words, God is not limited by space or time—everything created by God is in his presence (Psalm 139 v 7-10). To say that God is omnipotent means that truly nothing is too hard for the Lord (Jeremiah 32 v 17); he is all-powerful.

- **God is unchanging:** In a world that is continually changing, God remains the unchanging constant. God does not change in terms of who he is, and he does not change what he has willed to be (Numbers 23 v 19; Psalm 102 v 27; Malachi 3 v 6). God does not evolve, improve or need an update. He is the same God, yesterday, today, and forever (Hebrews 13 v 8).

- **God is holy:** Holiness refers to being set apart or separate. God is set apart from sin in that he is perfectly pure morally (Isaiah 6 v 1-3). He does not have even the faintest touch of sin. In fact, his eyes are too perfect to behold evil (Habakkuk 1 v 13). But not only is God morally pure and separate from sin; he is separate from everything! He is set apart in his being as God; he is different from us in his very nature.

■ **God is righteous**: God is a God of justice; he will always do what is right and pure (Deuteronomy 32 v 4). God declares what he considers righteous through what has been revealed in his word (Psalm 19 v 7-8; Daniel 9 v 14). Based upon God's righteousness, we can expect that God will not act in a way that would contradict his own character. For example, he cannot and will not do anything that would be unholy. To do so God would have to deny and contradict himself. This is impossible.

■ **God is good**: The Bible teaches us that God is good and that he only ever does what is good (Psalm 119 v 68). We have no higher standard of goodness than God himself (Mark 10 v 18). We must then be careful not to elevate a secondary standard above God to evaluate his goodness. Everything that God does is good because God is good. His goodness is a holy and righteous goodness.

■ **God is loving**: When we think about God's love, it's common to dwell on his love for his creation, but we should remember that God loved prior to

Genesis 1 v 1. Do you remember how Jesus prayed in John 17?

"Father, I desire that they also, whom you have given me, may be with me where I am, to see my glory that you have given me because you loved me before the foundation of the world."

John 17 v 24

Before God ever created a single person, he was delighting in love within the Trinity (Father, Son, and Holy Spirit). God is an eternally loving God. God loves himself and he loves his creation. There is little surprise then when we find the apostle John saying "God is love" (1 John 4 v 8).

God is jealous for his glory: Does it strike you as odd if I say that *God loves himself*? At first glance, you might be tempted to think this is somehow sinfully selfish. This would be a proper conclusion if God were anyone else but God. When you and I love ourselves, we are acting sinfully—we are being selfish. However, when God does this he is simply acting like God. Not to love himself would be a denial of his supremacy and a contradiction of his character. This is why we see God speaking about his jealous love for his glory throughout the Bible.

"I am the LORD; that is my name; I will not yield my glory to another or my praise to idols".

Isaiah 42 v 8

> "For my own sake, for my own sake, I do this. How can I let myself be defamed? I will not yield my glory to another."   *Isaiah 48 v 11*

> "You shall have no other gods before me."
> *Exodus 20 v 3*

God acts with a continual regard for the promotion of his glory.

When we think about hell, we have to begin with a proper understanding of who God is. I don't pretend to have exhausted the subject here, but rather, just to have set the table. To summarize: God has no beginning or end (he's eternal), is all-powerful and everywhere present (he's infinite), does not change, is morally pure and separate (he's holy), is consistently just (he's righteous), is always being and doing good, is loving, and is jealously committed to his own glory.

It is important to observe that at this point in the discussion there is no need for hell. We are simply talking about who God is. In other words, hell is not essential to God's character. However, hell is the *essential response* of God's character to sin.

A statement like this requires thoughtful consideration not only of God's character but also of human sin. If the Bible teaches that sin warrants such a punishment as hell, then we must be certain we understand that correctly also.

✕

What is sin?

Look around today, and you would get a very different impression of what sin is from how it is described in the Bible.

Sin does not make us blush as it did people in generations past. Instead mention of the word is considered wise marketing, because most people are attracted by sin, rather than repelled by it. Some speak fondly of Las Vegas as "Sin-City." I've seen apparel in mainline clothing stores with sin creatively drawn into the design to be paraded about by customers.

In my own city there is a restaurant that markets itself with the word. *Sinful Burger* boasts of its "evilly delicious" hamburgers. In this restaurant, where "being bad never tasted so good" you can enjoy burgers named Greed, Lust, Pride, and Sloth. If you are really up for a sinful challenge, there is the massive Hades burger. If you were to speak of sin in terms that communicate moral accountability you would often be met with surprised looks. Any implication that we have sinned and deserve consequences is considered both antiquated and priggish.

One reason for the dilution of the concept of sin is that our contemporary understanding of it has been relativized. We think that sin is what *really bad people do*. Sin is for people like Hitler, Stalin, and members of ISIS. It is for the demonstrably bad and universally-agreed-upon reprobates. I read of a well-known family who had just tragically lost their son in a car accident. While they were at a televised public event speaking about their loss, their home was robbed. In reporting the news, a journalist noted that there was "a special place in hell" reserved for people that took advantage of others like this.

It is strange what we think about hell and sin. On the one hand it makes us laugh and feel better about ourselves, and on the other hand it reassures us that bad people will be properly punished. In this common scenario of how sin is thought and talked about, there are two people who are completely removed from the discussion—*God* and *us*. This is why we must allow the Bible to properly shape our understanding of what sin is, and how it strikes deeply into our own hearts.

What does the Bible teach about sin?

Sin is used in a number of different ways in the Bible. In perhaps the most well-known verse, it is described as **missing the mark**:

> ...for all have sinned and fall short of the glory of
> God.   *Romans 3 v 23*

The mark is God's standard of obedience to his word; all have fallen short, and we have missed the mark. Like an archer failing to hit the center of a target, humanity has completely missed—it has buried itself in the ground, pathetically short of the mark.

Sin is also described as **crossing the line**. The word used here is "trespasses":

> And you, who were dead in your trespasses ... God
> made alive together with him, having forgiven us
> all our trespasses.   *Colossians 2 v 13* (ESV)

As a fence around a property defines a boundary, so God's word lays out for us God's boundaries of right and wrong; good and bad; healthy and unhealthy; what leads to life and what leads to death. When we sin, we are trespassing across God's defined boundaries for his creation.

In a succinct definition, the apostle John describes sin as **breaking God's law**,

Sin is lawlessness.   *1 John 3 v 4*

Quite literally, this word translated "lawlessness" means "against the law." Sin is acting against God's law. When we sin we not only break his law, but we show that we do not care for about it.

Sin is also described as **a debt**. Jesus uses this term in what we know as the Lord's Prayer. He instructs his followers to pray to the Father requesting forgiveness from their debts (Matthew 6 v 12). The word for debt can be used to express a financial obligation (Romans 4 v 4). This concept is common to every age, and Jesus deploys it here to express our obligation in a moral sense. Our sin puts us in debt to God, and the price needs to be paid.

We can summarize the Bible's teaching on sin by asking three questions that lead us to a fourth.

- *Who sins?* The Bible is clear that every single person that has ever lived has sinned. We are sinners by nature (Ephesians 2 v 1) and by action (Ephesians 2 v 2-3).

- *How do we sin?* We sin by not obeying God's word.

- *Who do we sin against?* While sin can and often does have interpersonal implications, it is primarily against God (Psalm 51 v 4).

Sin then is what all people do when they break God's law in rebellion against him. The fourth question is this: *What are the inevitable consequences?*

In this discussion of the reason for hell, we have observed that the issues of who God is and what sin is are central. So far we have briefly looked at both. Now let's put them together and see how they connect and inform our understanding of hell.

God's goodness requires justice

Do you remember my barber's objection to the biblical doctrine of hell? His contention was that a good God could not possibly send people to hell. This comment is remarkably perceptive. While I think he came to the wrong conclusion, I do believe he put his finger on a central issue. The discussion about the reason for hell pivots on the goodness of God and the sinfulness of humanity. How good is God? And, how bad are we?

Let me put it another way. I don't think that it's the biblical teaching of hell that puts people off, instead it's the gospel. People are offended by what the Bibles says about what our sin is and what it deserves in light of God's character. I realize this is a radical thought, but hell is not nearly as offensive as God's holiness, goodness, and love for his own glory.

Think with me about an earthly judge. Let's suppose there is a judge who is hearing the case of a corporate executive who has embezzled millions of dollars and cheated his co-workers out of their life savings and pensions. The judge listens to hours of testimony from weeping and ruined victims. The facts of the case are undeniable. But after all has been said, he declares the executive to be "not guilty." In pronouncing the judgment, he smiles warmly at the defendant and says, "Congratulations, you're free to go."

We can imagine the scene. The court would be in an uproar, and eventually the judge would be asked very hard questions, and likely removed from office. But consider the even greater outrage when, upon being asked why he let the despicable criminal go, he said, "Because I'm a good judge." Nobody would agree with the judge's assessment.

In a case where someone is clearly guilty, declaring them to be "not guilty" is a gross miscarriage of justice. No matter how good the judge may think he is, by letting the guilty man free he proves that he is not good. He is bad, unjust, and despicable. There would be justifiable speculation about whether he was on the take, perhaps even accepting a bribe from the wealthy defendant. It would be universally agreed that this judge is anything but good.

How is it that so many have such a different understanding of goodness when we talk about God? Most people acknowledge (even if reluctantly) that they are imperfect in God's sight. Many will even agree that they have sinned. But to say that they deserve hell—this is too far. They are holding God to a standard of goodness that is below that to which they would hold a local judge.

A good God

One of the reasons for this is because people think of goodness in terms of the good *that they receive*. I think you are good to the extent that you are good *to me*. If God judges sin, then that is not good for me.

But when we read the Bible, we have to understand God's goodness in terms of God's own character. God's goodness is consistent with his holiness, righteousness, and love. And this goodness is characterized by a jealousy for his own glory. While many appeal to God's goodness as the reason why they don't believe that God will send people to hell, it's actually a major reason for it. God's goodness *requires* justice; it never condones injustice.

This is similar to how God's love is portrayed. We think of God's love as him making a big deal *about us*. But what if the Bible showed us that God's love for us is actually all about making a big deal *about himself*—by rescuing people who weren't all that impressive? When we read in John 3 v 16 that "God so loved the world that he gave his one and only Son", we should be impressed by God's love, not because the world is *so big*, but because it is *so bad*.

When we are thinking about who God is, we must remember that his attributes are not in conflict within him. God does not compromise his holiness in order to accommodate his love. His attributes are not at odds with one another. The proper expression of God's goodness is the punishment of evil. The Bible shows us that what makes sin so evil is that it is against God; it is the highest offense (Psalm 51 v 4). Sin is the greatest evil precisely because of who it is against.

Who rules hell?

Growing up I got my theology the same place most kids got it: cartoons. Watching a show like *Tom & Jerry* helped to shape my understanding of hell. Upon the untimely "death" of Tom, he would find himself in the flames of hell under the rule of a devilish despot armed with a pitchfork and unsettling horns. My conclusion: hell is ruled by the devil.

Is Satan the governor of hell? The Bible teaches us that hell is not only a real place but also a real place *created by God*. While we don't have the GPS location of hell, we do have many Bible verses that testify to its existence and the fact that it was God who created it. *But who was it created for?*

We read in Matthew's Gospel that Jesus says this:

> "Then he will say to those on his left, 'Depart from me, you who are cursed, into the eternal fire prepared for the devil and his angels'."
>
> *Matthew 25 v 41*

Hell is ruled by *God*, not Satan. It will be the final destination of Satan, the fallen angels, and all who finally reject God (see also Revelation 21 v 8; 14 v 10; Philippians 2 v 10)—it is the dustbin for all that is evil in the world. Therefore, we could say that hell was not a part of God's good creation but was created as a consequence of the rebellion within God's creation.

This is important to understand. To say that God is a judge, or that he is angry against sin is different from saying that God is love. God is love because there has always been someone to love from eternity. At the heart of the universe is a triune God—Father, Son, and Holy Spirit—bound up in loving, joyous relationship with each other. We can confidently believe and say that at the very centre of the universe there is a relationship of pure love.

But God's anger, and the place where it is ultimately expressed—hell—is different. His wrath has been called into existence as a response to sin and rebellion in his world. God is love. He is not hate or anger or wrath. He hates sin. He is angry at sinful rebels. He will express his anger in wrathful judgment. But all the while he is love. But while God's judgment is both right and just, there is no joy in it:

> "Do I take any pleasure in the death of the
> wicked? declares the Sovereign LORD. Rather, am I
> not pleased when they turn from their ways and
> live?"   *Ezekiel 18 v 23*

> "As surely as I live," declares the Sovereign LORD,
> "I take no pleasure in the death of the wicked,
> but rather that they turn from their ways and live

Turn! Turn from your evil ways! Why will you die,
people of Israel?"   *Ezekiel 33 v 11*

What's the point?

Does the punishment fit the crime?

There is at least one nagging question raised by
getting a handle on the reason for hell. What exactly
does it accomplish? What is the point in having a place
inhabited by an uncomfortably large number of people
suffering judgment throughout all eternity? Doesn't it
all seem a little, well, pointless?

It's normal for us to begin to reason through this question with reference to our natural dealings with other
people. When a citizen breaks the law, he receives a
punishment that fits the crime. Someone would not get
a life sentence for speeding, dropping litter in the street
or jaywalking. This is common for us in all types of relationships—parents disciplining their children, bosses
dealing with their subordinates, and so on. Indeed, it is
a principle of justice that comes from the Bible itself: an
eye for an eye, a tooth for a tooth (Exodus 21:24). The
punishment *must* fit the crime.

But while this is a common reflex, it should prompt
us to consider if this is the right comparison to make.
Are we really comparing like with like here? Or are we
confusing apples with oranges? While the Bible teaches
that the punishment should fit the crime, it also explains why such a severe punishment as hell fits the
crime of sin. The Bible presents hell as a just penalty
for sin.

Why sin is so bad

Imagine walking down the street and you notice someone sitting on a bench focused on what's in his hands. Unable to see, you peer in closer and observe that he is pulling the legs off a grasshopper.

How would you respond?

Other than thinking him to be a bit strange you more than likely wouldn't confront him about what he is doing. It's cruel, sure, but we swat insects everyday without much of a second thought. But what if it wasn't a grasshopper but a frog? You would likely be a bit more disturbed, but perhaps also reluctant to stop and confront the stranger.

And what if it was a bird? Would you say something then? Would you call the police?

How about if it was a puppy? Sensing the instability and malevolence of the man, you might refrain from confrontation but you would definitely call the authorities.

Finally, what if it was a human baby? Would you stop him? Would you intervene? *No question*. At risk to yourself you would intervene and physically fight him to protect the child.

What is the difference in each of these scenes? Why would most people keep walking if they saw a grasshopper, but stop if they saw a child being assaulted? What prompts a different reaction? In each case the act is the same—pulling off legs. What's the difference? *It's the one who is sinned against.*

Your response would be different in the face of the same action depending upon the value of the one who is being sinned against. The more valuable the creature, the more serious and reprehensible it is to assault them. If God were a grasshopper, then eternal, conscious punishment would be an overreaction. But God is not a grasshopper.[1]

The God of the Bible is perfect in holiness, righteousness and love. There is no one who compares with him in terms of his beauty. In fact, his beauty is an infinite beauty. His glory is of infinite worth. He deserves perfection. He is worthy of this. Anything less than this perfection is not a misdemeanor but a capital offense. Eternal hell corresponds with the nature of God and the nature of sin. Since God is the highest good, then sin against him is the highest form of evil. The punishment of an eternal hell corresponds with the worth of an infinitely glorious God.

Misconceptions about hell will always err on these two points: the worth of God and the sinfulness of sin. God's worth corresponds with sin's punishment. Nobody gets upset over the loss of something of little value, but if those things are of high value, then everyone can see their importance. If we don't see sin as an attack on God's infinite worth, then we will not see hell as a just response to it. The punishment does indeed fit the crime.

But why must it be forever?

God made humans to be eternal beings. As God is

---

1   This helpful illustration is from Denny Burk in *Four Views on Hell* (Zondervan, 2016) p. 18-19.

eternal so he has made his image bearers to exist forever. Jesus shows that all of us will exist in one of two places, but both will be an eternal, conscious existence:

> "And they will go away to eternal punishment, but the righteous to eternal life."
>
> *Matthew 25 v 46*

But the duration of hell is not simply because of how we were made, but because of what we have done. Sin incurs an infinite debt. Hell is simply God expressing his character throughout all eternity. As unsettling as it might be, each day in hell is a sermon that declares the infinite value of God's glory. Hell says, "God's holiness does not compromise. God's love is not open to a bribe. God's righteousness is wonderfully inflexible. God's goodness is a perfect goodness."

Hell is also God's eternal repudiation of sin and declaration of his ongoing opposition to it. The ongoing punishment of sin in hell is God's ongoing opposition to all that opposes him. Because sin is against God, its debt takes on an eternal dimension. The debt sin incurs is an eternal debt. The eternal nature of hell declares both the infinite debt of sin and the infinite worth of God's glory.

As odd as it might at first appear, hell gives God glory as his righteous standard is upheld throughout all eternity in the punishment of all that opposes him. This expression of divine wrath in hell is the expression of his jealousy for his glory and his intolerance for anything that belittles it.

This is also the reason why the Bible writers are clear that it is a place of no return. Some think that people can work their way out of hell in some kind of way. Others suggest that hell is only "locked on the inside" and that people prevent themselves from getting out, by persisting in their rebellion against God. I'll speak to those questions in more detail in the Frequently Asked Questions pages at the end. But suffice it to say for the moment, the evidence of scripture is that, whether or not it is locked on the inside, God has firmly locked hell from the outside.

My barber put his finger squarely on the pulse of the issue. The central issues that must be discussed when considering the reason for hell are the character of God and what his reaction to human sin will be. If God is serious about his glory, then we can expect hell to be severe. In the Bible we see both to be true.

Thankfully, this is not the last word on the topic.

Chapter 4

Please… don't go to hell

As I stood leaning on the railing that overlooked Niagara Falls, I was struck by the sheer volume of the water relentlessly flowing over the edge. As far as it depended upon me, it was unstoppable. We could easily feel the same way when we contemplate the reality of eternal judgment. There are so many people in the world. Is there anything that I can do to help them escape hell? Or am I helpless?

Thankfully there is something that I can do. There is a way—only one way—to escape hell. I can tell you about it. And, if you haven't done so already, you can believe the message and find the answer to the biggest question of life: what can I do about my sin?

Home with God

In the very beginning of the Bible, we find a God who loves to make things big and beautiful. The entire world was created by God and for God (Colossians 1 v 16). The continual refrain in chapter one of Genesis as creation unfolds echoes God's approval: "And God saw that it was good." It's as if God steps back from what he has made in admiration, saying repeatedly, *"This is wonderful!"* Indeed it was—indeed it *is.*

The jewel of God's creation is humanity. God gave people the distinct privilege of being made in his image (Genesis 1 v 26-27). As image-bearers, we are rational and relational. We are able to speak and relate in a way that is wholly different from the rest of creation. Furthermore, we are spiritual beings who are imprinted with a copy of many of God's attributes. Among these, we have a sense of justice, love, and mercy. God has designed us with these moral attributes so that we would relate to him in worship, and reflect him in our relationships with the rest of creation. As soon as they were created, humanity was home with God, and a perfect reflection of God. In other words, we loved and glorified him perfectly.

A (sin) broken home

Speaking to his new image-bearers, God gave them free reign in his freshly minted creation. He only included one stipulation: *Don't eat from the tree of the knowledge of good and evil* (Genesis 2 v 17). In a world filled with beautiful trees and delicious fruit, God marked out this one tree and said it was off limits. In addition to the prohibition for the tree, God provided a loving, clear warning: "For when you eat of it you will certainly die" (Genesis 2 v 17). The message is clear: *Obey me and live; disobey and die.*

Soon after, Adam and Eve were tempted by Satan to eat from this tree. They were unable to resist their own urge to taste the fruit and sink their teeth into the phantom promise of fulfillment. And because God is holy, good, and just, he judged them. They were cast out of the beautiful garden (Genesis 3 v 23). When Adam and Eve sinned, they incurred God's judgment. From here, things changed. Instead of a close relationship with God characterized by intimacy and peace, they were alienated and unsettled. The beautiful home of our first parents was broken by sin. We are all children of a broken home.

The sentence of death

God said that when the fruit of this tree was eaten, then they would die. What did God mean by "die" in Genesis 2? Adam and Eve clearly ate the fruit but did not immediately drop down dead. So in what sense *did* they die? How could they continue living if they were promised death? Many have found it helpful to divide the answers to this question into three different categories: spiritual, physical, and eternal death.

Spiritual death

Spiritual death refers to separation from God. When Adam and Eve sinned, they hid from God. Patching together a shield of fig leaves to mask their shame, they hid themselves from the presence of God (Genesis 3 v 7-8). Previously they had walked with God and enjoyed the sweetness of their relationship with him. But now, because of sin, their relationship was broken. It was changed. They died spiritually. The apostle Paul speaks to this when he writes of the condition of all people apart from Christ:

> You were dead in your transgressions and sins.
>
> *Ephesians 2 v 1*

This deadness is not physical but spiritual—we are dead to God. We can tell this by the corresponding deeds:

> ... in which you used to live when you followed the ways of this world and of the ruler of the kingdom of the air, the spirit who is now at work in those who are disobedient. All of us also lived among them at one time, gratifying the cravings of our flesh and following its desires and thoughts. Like the rest, we were by nature deserving of wrath.
>
> *Ephesians 2 v 2-3*

To be spiritually dead is to live to that which opposes God, and be dead to that which ultimately pleases him. It is to have our understanding darkened (Ephesians 4 v 18), and to be unable and unwilling to please God.

When Adam and Eve sinned, they died *spiritually*. The spiritual death of humanity became the new normal after that fateful day in the garden. All the offspring of Adam and Eve (including you and me) were born alienated from God (see Colossians 1 v 21; Psalm 51 v 5; Romans 3 v 10-18, 23).

Physical death

Prior to Adam and Eve's sin in Genesis 3 there was no death. Everything was living and not dying. Can you imagine that? However, upon the first sin, death was ushered into this world (Romans 5 v 12).

Right after the narrative about Adam and Eve's diso-bedience, there is the story of their children: Cain and Abel. Tragically, Cain murders his younger brother in a fit of jealous anger. Then Genesis Chapter 5 dramati-cally underscores the change with a genealogy that in-cludes the following pattern: birth, the number of years lived, and then the age of death. The refrain is clear—we are born, live for a time and then die.

This was not God's ideal in creation. He created this world for his glory and human flourishing. We were to enjoy him and his blessings throughout eternity. However, sin brought death. This pattern has continued right down to our current day.

Cemeteries testify that death is a persistent hound that eventually, inevitably, runs down its quarry. We cannot escape it by any means. Physical death will one day claim us all and testify that we too are children of the first man and woman who fell in the garden of Eden.

Eternal death

The third aspect of death is referred to as eternal death. This has to do with the eternal sentence of hell. The Bible also calls this the "second death" (Revelation 21 v 8). The first death refers to the spiritual and physical while the second death is in the eternal lake of fire. This coincides with all that we have been talking about in this book.

When we put these three aspects of death together, we can see that the promised judgment of death is mul-ti-faceted. We have all died spiritually. We will certainly all die physically. However, eternal death is the matter that we are concerned with here. We do not have to die in this way. We do not need to go to hell.

Jesus rescues people from hell

Recently, I had the joy of sitting down with my parents and my son to go through an old collection of family papers and pictures. Inside the box were pictures from the late 19th century. As we eagerly sifted through the contents, we found my grandfather's handwritten notes about our family tree. He had spent hours and hours researching his family history, and putting it on paper so that future generations would have a record of it. We could sense the curiosity and joy that fueled his research. It's important for us to know where we come from.

It's interesting that we, who can be so interested in family trees, so often skip over the genealogies in the Bible. These records serve to show us that the Bible is about the lives of real people, just like you and me.

And when we read the genealogies, we discover there is a profound theological importance that must not be skipped over. In the Gospel of Luke we read the genealogy of Jesus. It works back through dozens of names from Joseph, back to King David, and Judah and Abraham, until we find ourselves face to face with the first man— Adam (Luke 3 v 23-38).

What is the point of this connection to Adam? Is it simply to showcase the precise record-keeping of the ancient world? Not at all. The importance of this connection to Adam is to show us, the readers, that Jesus has come as a descendant of Adam. He is the offspring of Adam and Eve. He is fully man. But he is a unique man.

Unlike Adam (and every one of us throughout history), Jesus never sinned. He was sinless and perfect (2 Corinthians 5 v 21; 1 Peter 2 v 22). This means that when Christ was faced with all of the temptations and difficulties that we face as people, he never gave in—he never sinned (Hebrews 4 v 15). Immediately after the genealogy in Luke 3, we read of Jesus facing temptation in the wilderness. Given the same choice that was presented to Adam and Eve by the serpent, the Lord Jesus trusted God and his word, and rejected Satan with these words:

> *"It is written: 'Worship the Lord your God and serve him only.'"*   Luke 4 v 8

The test that the first man and woman failed so decisively, the Lord Jesus Christ passed with flying colors and continued to pass each day of his life.

Remember the requirement God placed on all creation? He commanded that all people obey him perfectly. This is exactly what Jesus did in his life. He could say, with reference to his Father:

> "The one who sent me is with me; he has not left me alone, for I always do what pleases him."
> John 8 v 29

> "My food ... is to do the will of him who sent me and to finish his work."   John 4 v 34

The obedience of Jesus to his Father was not a chore. It wasn't a burden or an unpleasant task. Hebrews 10 quotes Psalm 40 by saying "I desire to do your will, my

God; your law is within my heart" (v 8). It wasn't simply a mechanical external duty; it was an internal delight to obey his Father. Little wonder then that his Father, on multiple occasions, would interrupt the day's events by thundering a shout from heaven with a declaration that "This is my Son whom I love, with him I am well pleased" (Matthew 3 v 17; 17 v 5).

Why did Jesus do this? He delighted to do God's will, but he wasn't doing it for his own pleasure. He was doing it for people like you and me—the offspring of Adam and Eve.

How does this work? Jesus lived as our representative and substitute. He lived in our place. The life that you and I should have lived was one of perfect obedience to God's word (loving him and others perfectly). Jesus came and said, *I will live for her. I will obey for her. I will be perfect in her place.* Through his perfect obedience to God's law Jesus earned righteousness—the basis of acceptance before God.

But this is not all.

We have seen that the "wages of sin is death" (Romans 6 v 23). Since we have sinned we've earned death. Because Jesus is our substitute, he has taken on the responsibility of paying our debt. He died in our place. He took our punishment. He paid the penalty due to us for our sins:

> He was delivered up for our sins and raised to life for our justification.   *Romans 4 v 25*

> For I delivered to you as of first importance what

> For what I received I passed on to you as of first importance: that Christ died for our sins according to the Scriptures... *1 Corinthians 15 v 3*

> He himself bore our sins in his body on the cross, so that we might die to sins and live for righteousness; by his wounds you have been healed.*1 Peter 2 v 24*

> ...and from Jesus Christ who is the faithful witness, the firstborn from the dead, and the ruler of the kings of the earth. To him who loves us and has freed us from our sins by his blood. *Revelation 1 v 5*

The genealogy is very important. Jesus came for people like you and me. He came to seek and save the lost children of Adam and make them children of God. He came to rescue people from hell by delivering them from the wrath to come (1 Thessalonians 1 v 10).

Jesus suffered hell on earth

About 15 years ago the movie *The Passion of Christ* was extremely popular. The filmmakers attempted to portray the gruesome nature of crucifixion. The torture endured by Christ was shown in the movie in intense detail, and the point was clearly made: Jesus suffered immensely at the hands of his accusers.

But if this is all we see when we consider the cross of Christ, then we have not seen it fully. The night before Jesus was betrayed, he was in deep agony in Gethsemane. He said, "My soul is overwhelmed with sorrow to the point of death..." (Matthew 26 v 38). In Luke's

Gospel we read that his agony was so intense that as he prayed earnestly, he sweated drops of blood (22 v 44). Was it the prospect of human torture that drove Christ to this agony? Was Jesus in agony at the prospect of dying for his faith? Was he dreading martyrdom?

We learn the answer in his prayer. His agony centered on a cup.

> Going a little farther, he fell with his face to the ground and prayed, "My Father, if it is possible, may this cup be taken from me. Yet not as I will, but as you will."   *Matthew 26 v 39*

The object of Christ's attention here is this cup. What is the cup? What's in it? In Scripture the cup refers to God's wrath or judgment (Isaiah 51 v 17; Jeremiah 25 v 15). Here in this foreboding vessel before Jesus is the fully fermented, undiluted cup of divine wrath. It is God's impending judgment that has him sweating drops of blood and in deep agony. Christ is looking down the barrel of heaven's infinite wrath and his heart is shredded in agony. As barbaric as the human suffering was, it was not the chief agony of the cross. This was reserved for his assignment to drink the cup. It wasn't the prospect of martyrdom—wrath at the hands of men—that weighed so heavily upon Jesus; it was the wrath of God.

A short time after this episode in Gethsemane, Jesus was arrested, tried, and sentenced to be crucified on a wooden cross. The cross became an altar of sacrifice. Jesus offered himself as a sacrifice for the sins of the people. What did the sacrifice of Christ aim to accomplish? It was to pay the debt for our sin by satisfying God's wrath. The theological word for this is "propitiation." On the cross Jesus satisfied God's just, holy, and good wrath against our sin. And by bearing the wrath fully required for sinners, Jesus makes God propitious or favorable toward us (Romans 3 v 25; Hebrews 2 v 17).

Consider it. On the cross Jesus suffered and endured the full weight of God's holy anger. He took the full weight of an eternal hell compressed and tamped down. Jesus proclaimed upon his last breath, "It is finished" (John 19 v 30). *What is finished?* Among other things, he finished his work of satisfying the wrath of God. He suffered hell on earth. He emptied the cup. As Charles Spurgeon says, "He drank damnation dry."

The rescue

We have thought a bit about how consistent God is. He is faithful to act consistently with who he is; he'll never contradict himself. So let's consider how this works, specifically with regard to people being rescued from the penalty of sin.

When Jesus came, he came as a substitute for sinners like you and me. His whole life was a substitution. But when Jesus went to the cross, he was specifically satisfying God's wrath for us. The righteous suffered in the place of the unrighteous.

Jesus was treated as if he had broken God's law and deserved judgment, so that God could treat us as if we had obeyed God's law perfectly and deserve blessings:

God made him who had no sin to be sin for us, so that in him we might become the righteousness of God.   *2 Corinthians 5 v 21*

For Christ also suffered once for sins, the righteous for the unrighteous, to bring you to God. He was put to death in the body but made alive in the Spirit.   *1 Peter 3 v 18*

Christ redeemed us from the curse of the law by becoming a curse for us, for it is written: "Cursed is everyone who is hung on a pole." He redeemed us in order that the blessing given to Abraham might come to the Gentiles through Christ Jesus, so that by faith we might receive the promise of the Spirit.
                    Galatians 3 v 13-14

We receive this blessing by turning from our sin and trusting in Jesus. We renounce our sin by confessing it to God and turning from it in repentance. We believe in Jesus not simply in the sense that we believe that he existed, but we believe in the sense that we trust in him and love him as our Savior.

God doesn't compromise—but he does save

Ever since I became a Christian, I have been struck time and again by God's love. God has, in his infinite wisdom, demonstrated his love to people who seemed completely hopeless. But notice how he does it: *he doesn't compromise*.

I remember my grandfather when I was young; he would catch me doing something wrong and would rarely get onto me about it. Instead, he would pat me on the behind, give me a piece of candy, and say, "Go play outside." God is not this way. He is not like a cosmic grandpa who sees us mess up, but doesn't have the heart to punish us. He doesn't look the other way. He can't. Instead he does something much more difficult—and painful.

In the gospel, God maintains the integrity of all of his attributes. His love, justice, holiness, and goodness are all on display in perfect harmony on the cross.

- *How do we know what love looks like?* Look at the cross (Romans 5 v 8).

- *What about righteousness?* Gaze upon Jesus as he died for our sins (Romans 3 v 25-26).

- *How holy is God?* Only the perfect blood of Christ could satisfy God's wrath and cleanse us from sin (1 Thessalonians 1 v 10; 1 John 1 v 7-9).

- *How good is God?* He punishes sin and saves sinners (Romans 3 v 26; Titus 2 v 11-14). God does not compromise his character; instead he demonstrates it through Christ on the cross—to the shock of men and angels.

Think about this: our sin has merited eternal death. We are helpless and hopeless to pay this debt; we are neither willing nor able to come up with the payment. But God in his infinite loving wisdom sends Jesus for us. He is both willing and able. Jesus is the eternal Son, who offered an eternal sacrifice, to satisfy God's eternal justice, and provide eternal life for people like you and me (Hebrews 9 v 14-15)! He suffered eternal hell in order to give us eternal life.

The urgency of the matter

One day the apostle Paul was talking to a bunch of people about Jesus. Some of the things he said to them struck them as curious, others as offensive. However, he wanted to make sure they understood the urgency of the matter. In concluding the sermon-like discussion he said this:

> "In the past God overlooked such ignorance, but now he commands all people everywhere to repent. For he has set a day when he will judge the world with justice by the man he has appointed. He has given proof of this to everyone by raising him from the dead."
>
> *Acts 17 v 30–31*

If the Bible were a newspaper, then the headline on the front-page would be one of warning. It warns us all to repent of our sins and trust in Christ. The reason is that God has fixed a day in which he will finally judge the world—and all people in it. We don't have a say in the matter. It is a fixed appointment on God's eternal calendar; it's going to happen. The only sensible response is repentance toward God and faith in the Lord Jesus Christ—anything else would be madness, given the stakes.

Too often, however, we lull ourselves back to spiritual sleep. Having been affected by a doctrine such as hell in a study, book or sermon, we are tempted to console ourselves for the discomfort we feel in our souls by dulling our conviction. Jesus told a story about a man who was planning on living a long time and enjoying all of his resources. As we finish this book, it's worth hearing the full force of what he says.

> And he told them this parable: "The ground of a certain rich man yielded an abundant harvest. He thought to himself, 'What shall I do? I have no place to store my crops.' Then he said, 'This is what I'll do. I will tear down my barns and build bigger ones, and there I will store my surplus grain. And I'll say to myself, 'You have plenty of grain laid up for many years. Take life easy; eat, drink and be merry.' But God said to him, 'You fool! This very night your life will be demanded from you. Then who will get what you have prepared for yourself?'"
> *Luke 12 v 16-20*

What if tonight your life is demanded of you? What if tonight, the soul was required of your friend, your spouse, your neighbor?

Friend, our sin will certainly be dealt with. God will not compromise his character; either our sin will be punished with hell by Jesus on the cross, or in hell by you forever. But be in no doubt about this—it *will be punished*.

Therefore, I plead with you: as painful as this subject may be, do not let your convictions be dulled, but cry out to those you know and those you meet. Plead with them, "Don't go to hell. It is real. It was not made for you, but it waits for you, because you deserve it. And even though the One who is good and righteous and holy will justly send you there, he has also provided the only way out. So turn to Christ and be gloriously and wonderfully welcomed into the embrace of his nail-pierced hands."

Alternative views on hell

While Christians have enjoyed considerable agreement on the biblical teaching of hell throughout church history, there are some who maintain alternative views. The issues at hand are whether or not there is actual punishment and, if so, how long it lasts. I will interact with each view briefly and provide what I believe to be a biblical response to it.

1. Universalism

Universalism is the view that all people will ultimately be saved and none will experience God's judgment. Proponents of this view point to the following Scriptural passages for support:

> Consequently, just as one trespass resulted in condemnation for all people, so also one righteous act resulted in justification and life for all people.
>
> *Romans 5 v 18*

> For as in Adam all die, also in Christ all will be made alive. *1 Corinthians 15 v 22*

Another passage that is frequently used to support a universalist position is in Paul's first letter to the Corinthians. Paul is looking ahead to the end of the age and the consummation of all things.

> Then the end will come, when he hands over the kingdom to God the Father after he has destroyed all dominion, authority and power. For he must reign until he has put all his enemies under his feet. The last enemy to be destroyed is death. For he "has put everything under his feet." Now when it says that "everything" has been put under him, it is clear that this does not include God himself, who put everything under Christ. When he has done this, then the Son himself will be made subject to him who put everything under him, so that God may be all in all.
>
> *1 Corinthians 15 v 24-28*

Universalists pack their view into the declaration that "God may be all in all." They conclude that this indicates that God works to save people after they die.

A quick review of 1 Corinthians 15, however, would find that the enjoyment of God's blessing from the gospel is only for those who put *active faith* in Christ. Paul's recurring reminder in this chapter is that our faith is not useless or futile but absolutely vital (v 12-19). It is by faith that we lay hold of the resurrection and eternal life. The necessity of faith in Christ is a casualty of universalism's sentimentality.

The universalist's contention that these passages

support their doctrine should seem to have some cracks in it. Rather than referring to every single person who ever lived, the phrase "all people" in Romans 1 v 18 and 1 Corinthians 15 v 22 refers to all the people who receive Christ. This is clear from the context of Romans:

> For if, because of one man's trespass, death reigned through that one man, much more will those who receive the abundance of grace and the free gift of righteousness reign in life through the one man Jesus Christ. *Romans 5 v 17*

It is incumbent upon us to receive this abundant grace in Christ. The entire flow of the context of Romans has been emphasizing the need for faith in Christ. All are under sin and deserving of God's wrath (chapters 1 – 3) but God in his grace has justified his people freely in Christ (3 v 24 – 5 v 11).

One thing that flows from being justified now is that we can be certain we have peace with God (5 v 1), and will certainly be saved from the coming wrath of God (5 v 9). This is why we "rejoice in God through our Lord Jesus Christ" (5 v 11, ESV).

Further, if universalism were true, it would make little sense for Paul to have "great sorrow and unceasing anguish" in his heart for his unbelieving Jewish kinsmen (Romans 9 v 1-5). Why is he so worked up about their unbelief if, in the end, they will be recipients of God's love and not his wrath?

On the contrary, "since the we know what it is to fear the Lord, we try to persuade others..." (2 Corinthians 5 v 11).

The certainty of salvation for all people—regardless of what they believe about Jesus and the gospel—actually discourages evangelism. But the certainty of the coming judgment compels a believer to faithful evangelism.

It is hard to resist the conclusion that the arguments in favor of universalism are not primarily biblical but *sentimental*. They lean heavily on the (true) belief that God loves people, but cannot accept that such love is consistent with an eternal hell. The Bible is clear that after death comes judgment:

> And just as it is appointed for man to die once, and after that comes judgment...*Hebrews 9 v 27*, ESV

The parable that Jesus told of the rich man and Lazarus likewise teaches that there are no second chances after death (Luke 16 v 19-31).

There is a real distaste for the reality of hell in those drawn to universalism—and I can completely relate to this. The thought that a huge number of people will suffer for an incalculably long time is difficult to take in. Those who can find no other way to read Jesus' teaching, and therefore embrace the reality of an eternal, conscious punishment in hell, should not lack compassion.

But there is a big difference between having compassion and manipulating the word of God. In a strange twist of irony, universalists are motivated by love for other people, but reveal a shocking lack of love for God and his Word—and therefore ultimately for other people. If the gospel is the only thing that can save people, but they abandon the importance of sharing the gospel, they are actually failing to love others as Christ loves them. To quote again the most famous verse in the Bible:

> For God so loved the world that he gave his one and only Son, that whoever believes in him shall not perish but have eternal life.   *John 3 v 16*

His love is for the world, yes. But his salvation is only for those who believe in him.

2. Annihilationism

Annihilationism teaches that unbelievers are punished for their sins for a time after their death, but then they are destroyed or annihilated so that they no longer exist.

Annihilationism is closely related to something theologians call "conditional immortality"; The two phrases are often, but not always, used interchangeably. Conditional immortality maintains that the only people who will live forever in eternity are those who are Christians. In this view, those who reject Christ will cease to exist upon their death or at the time of judgment. People are only "potentially" immortal. Proponents of this view hold that only God is immortal (1 Timothy 6 v 16), and that when we become Christians, we become partakers of the divine nature (2 Peter 1 v 4).

While this view has been gaining increased attention in recent years, it is not new. It was rejected at the second Council of Constantinople (AD 553). Some modern proponents of this view include the Jehovah's Witnesses and Seventh-day Adventists. But it is not limited to those who hold views on other matters that are outside the mainstream of orthodoxy. It seems to be gaining influence in our day. Some of the main arguments are included and answered below.

The first issue that is raised is the duration of hell. Will it last forever? Is it eternal? In Mark 9 v 43-48 we twice read what Jesus said about unquenchable fire— a clear reference to hell. The urgent call for action is weighted by both the eternal duration and the torment in hell.

> If your hand causes you to stumble, cut it off. It is better for you to enter life maimed than with two hands to go into hell, where the fire never goes out. And if your foot causes you to stumble, cut it off. It is better for you to enter life crippled than to have two feet and be thrown into hell. And if your eye causes you to stumble, pluck it out. It is better for you to enter the kingdom of God with one eye than to have two eyes and be thrown into hell, where 'the worms that eat them do not die, and the fire is not quenched.'   *Mark 9 v 43–48*

Annihilationists argue that the word "eternal" in the New Testament can sometimes refer to the finality of a matter rather than an unending process. Therefore, the reference to "eternal" here is simply a reference to the age to come when spoken with finality. Some examples include: "eternal salvation" (Hebrews 5 v 9); "eternal judgment" (6 v 2); "eternal redemption" (9 v 12); and "eternal punishment" (Matthew 25 v 46). If these examples simply referred to the age to come, then we would still be left with the question: How long *is* the age to come? A plain reading of the Bible text indicates that the point of contrasting eternal judgment alongside eternal life is to show how the two correlate. There is no indication that either the eternal blessing or eternal justice will cease—they will go on for ever.

Connected to this question for annihilationists is the use of the term "destruction." In passages that refer to destruction, those who hold this view understand it to mean extinction or annihilation. But this is not as convincing as it first sounds. Many commentators point out that in other passages where this word, or other similar terms are used, they don't refer to something ceasing to exist. Instead, they speak of a person or an object that is no longer functioning in the way it was designed to. Some examples include: wineskins that have holes in them (Matthew 9 v 17); a coin that's useless because it has been lost (Luke 15 v 9); or even the world itself that perished in the flood (2 Peter 3 v 6). In each of these examples the object still exists, but not in its originally designed way.

Another major issue with the traditional view of hell that annihilationists have is that they believe the idea of eternal punishment is inconsistent with the biblical view of God's love. As we considered in chapter 3 on the reason for hell, God's love is a jealous love and is characterized by holiness. God will not compromise his holiness in order to show love. Both hell and the cross demonstrate the seriousness of God on this matter; he is jealous for his glory.

While I share the sentiment that hell is disturbing, I cannot agree that the Bible teaches something other than eternal, conscious punishment. The arguments made by universalists and annihilationists are not biblically compelling. I believe that their attempt to resolve issues related to God's character and the nature of hell actually give raises more questions: How can God be just and loving? Does God's wrath ever really get satisfied? Why does God align eternal life alongside of eternal hell if the two don't correlate?"

All truth is one, and is interconnected. So these attempts to find a way out of the difficulties we have with the Bible's teaching on eternal punishment unwittingly diminish the sinfulness of sin, the character of God, the glory of Christ's atonement, and the call to take the gospel of God's grace and forgiveness to the ends of the earth.

Frequently asked questions about hell

When does a person go to hell?

We routinely use phrases to suggest that we experience hell as part of life. "His life was a living hell." "That place is hell on earth." Famously, the philosopher Jean Paul Sartre said, "Hell is other people", meaning that we are tormented by what other people think of us. As difficult as life is for many, the reality of hell is something of a far greater order than anything we may experience on earth.

But there are other questions about the "when" of hell. Do people go straight there after they die? At the second coming? Is there an Intermediate state? What is the timeline for judgment?

The Bible teaches that people die, and then after that comes the judgment (Hebrews 9 v 27). We do not read of second chances after death. The story of the rich man and Lazarus depicts intense suffering after death (Luke 16 v 19-31). And Jesus says to the thief at his crucifixion, "Today you will be with me in paradise" (Luke 23 v 43). It seems best to understand there is immediate punishment upon death, and then at the final judgment there is a resurrection of all for a final sentencing for all, either to everlasting life or everlasting punishment (Matthew 25 v 31-46).

Is there is an "intermediate" place like Limbo or Purgatory?

In the middle ages, a complex "geography" of hell was devised by the Catholic church. It included levels or circles of severity in punishment—as outlined in Dante's famous poem *The Divine Comedy*. But it also included the idea of an afterlife condition where souls may be purified before entering heaven. According to the catechism of the Roman Catholic Church, "All who die in God's grace and friendship, but still imperfectly purified, are indeed assured of their eternal salvation; but after death, they undergo purification, so as to achieve the holiness necessary to enter the joy of heaven." Two places of limbo are talked about: "The limbo of the Patriarchs" is a place where those who died before the coming of Jesus; and "The Limbo of the Infants"—a place where children and babies are held before being purified and welcomed into heaven.

The idea of Purgatory is common in the public imagination, as well as in the official teaching of Roman Catholic churches. The idea is that there is an intermediate place, where I get punished for the bad things I have done; after a suitable period of suffering, my soul is purified and I can enter heaven.

This idea, in all its forms, is completely at odds with the Bible's teaching about the gospel of grace. True, even if I have become a Christian by repenting and believing in Jesus, practically speaking, I am still less than perfect; I still sin. However, at the same time, positionally I have the righteousness of Christ immediately upon conversion, as it is charged to my account upon believing (Romans 5 v 1; 2 Corinthians 5 v 21). At the time of my death, the process of being made holy will be complete, and I will be fully sanctified and brought into the presence of God. Here I will, by the grace of God, be holy and blameless (1 Thessalonians 5 v 23; Jude v 24). When God forgives us, he forgives all of our sins: past, present, and future. I would see Purgatory as a teaching at odds not only with what the Bible says about the afterlife but also the very essence of Christianity—the gospel itself.

Who created hell? Why was hell created?

God created hell for the devil and the fallen angels (Matthew 25 v 41). This dispels the myth popularized by cartoons that the devil is in charge of hell with his red horns and pitchfork. Instead, we learn from the Scriptures that, in fact, God created and even rules hell as the righteous judge.

How long will hell last?

Hell will continue forever. It is eternal (Mark 9 v 43-48; Revelation 14 v 10-11; 20 v 10). Admittedly this reality is unsettling. However, we cannot escape the clear teaching of Scripture that hell is punishment for sin. And since the wages of sin is death, we must remember that an eternal hell is an eternal testimony to the display of God's righteousness.

How can you reconcile conflicting descriptions of hell?

I'll admit these descriptions are difficult to reconcile. Some have attempted to resolve the difference between darkness and the fire of hell by pointing out that the terms are metaphorical, depicting the twin truths of judgment and torment. If this is true, it doesn't disarm hell of its weight. Remember, picture language would communicate likeness to a reality that would likely be *far more intense* than the pictures used—we don't often use a metaphor to describe a lesser physical reality.

However, if these are literal terms indicating fire and darkness in tandem, there is the possibility that the intensity of the smoke in judgment could make everything dark. Either way darkness, and fire communicate banishment and judgment that is likely far worse than we could ever imagine.

Will people have the chance to repent in hell?

Jesus and the Bible in general give no indication of any opportunity to repent after death. There are no second chances. But not only are there no second chances; there is no indication of anyone *wanting* a second chance. The images we have of hell include anguish and suffering rather than contrition and pleading for forgiveness (Luke 16 v 19-31; Matthew 13 v 42).

How can hell be fair?

It's common for us to think about hell and other biblical doctrines from our natural, personal perspective. In contrast, the Bible urges us to see the world from a God-centered framework. We should not think of sin in terms of misdemeanors but rather, as capital offenses, since sin is primarily against God (Psalm 51 v 4)

The Scripture teaches that all of us have sinned and that sin deserves a just punishment. So is hell fair? Yes, because fair is getting what we deserve. However, I suspect that when many ask the question, they are wondering if hell is *warranted*. Since it is against God, sin is the highest offense. All sin is a high crime.

Is God really going to be that strict?

To understand the strictness of God, we must consider the cost he paid for people to avoid hell. The cross of Jesus Christ shows us what God thinks about sin and what it costs to pay for it. I believe hell corresponds with the penalty for sin and the costliness of Jesus' death on Calvary. God is just.

Is hell the expression of a loving God or an angry God?

Hell is God's just reaction to all who have not agreed with him about his glory. So yes, hell is God's wrath on display against sin. It is anger. But God's anger is fueled by a love for his glory and jealousy for his honor (Isaiah 42 v 8; 48 v 11). It is also an expression of his love for creation and for people. When we deliberately or carelessly hurt or harm others, or destroy God's good creation, we are destroying something that God loves. Just as any parent will be moved to anger at anyone who harms their child, so God, out of love for his creation, is righteously angry on behalf of those who are wounded by the sin of others.

If God has no pleasure in the death of the wicked, why will he send them to eternal torment?

God does not take pleasure in the destruction of the wicked. The Bible portrays God as patient (2 Peter 3 v 9). At the same time, he will receive glory from every single person that he has created, even if they refuse to give it. As shocking as it may be, the demonstration of justice in hell glorifies God because it upholds his righteousness even in the face of a lack of repentance (Romans 9 v 22-23).

Will God send people to hell who have never heard the gospel?

This is an important question for how we think about God and how we think about evangelism. It's important to remember that only sinners will be in hell. God will not send people to hell who have loved and obeyed him perfectly. We learn in Romans 1 v 18-20 that everyone has a knowledge of God written upon their hearts. They know who he is and what he deserves. But, while knowing this, we worship and serve the creation rather than the Creator. We don't need the gospel to show us this; creation testifies to it. Therefore, Paul argues in this important passage, we are all "without excuse" (Romans 1 v 20). This applies whether people have heard the gospel or not; we have ample revelation to condemn us before God. Second, the question implies (even if faintly) that it would be better for people *not* to hear the Gospel if it leads to condemnation. The reality of judgment is one of the major impulses for global missions. The reality of hell and the accountability of all people should fuel missions, not engender apathy.

In summary, nobody will be in hell because they have not heard the gospel, but because they have sinned. The fact that people have not heard should burden Christians to engage in reaching out to others with the gospel.

What about infants and the mentally disabled?

This is a hard question because the Bible does not appear to address it directly. There are ways in which we may draw some conclusions, but nothing definitively tells us one way or the other. In situations like this, we should find comfort by resting in God's character knowing that he will always do what is right (Genesis 18 v 25). I personally agree with many Bible teachers who believe that God saves, by his mysterious power and purpose, infants, young children, and the mentally disabled. I think it is right to give comfort and assurance to the parents of those who are incapable of making decisions. But our comfort must be in the goodness and justice of God. *He will do the right thing*, and when we come to the new creation ourselves, we will all agree that, whatever he has done, it is good and right and true, and we will rejoice in it.

Are there degrees of punishment in hell?

Jesus talked about a greater punishment for those listening to him who rejected him than for the people of Sodom who never saw him (Matthew 11 v 20-24). He also referred to one slave receiving greater punishment than another (Luke 12 v 47-48). While one sin is enough to incur God's wrath and make us guilty of breaking the entire law (James 2 v 10), there are some grounds for believing that the one who sins and never hears the gospel will go to hell, but their judgment will be of a lesser degree than the one who hears the gospel and refuses to repent of their sin. We do not know how this will happen, or how it will work in practice, but it reassures us that God's judgement will be appropriate and right for each person.

Will knowing that some of our loved ones are suffering in hell make it impossible for heaven to be pleasant?

It's healthy for us to feel the weight of hell upon us; this is especially true when considering those who are close to us. The apostle Paul modeled this when he wept and prayed in agony for his fellow countrymen (Romans 9 v 1-4). But we should not fear that our minds and hearts will be out of sync with the new creation. God will transform us perfectly into the image of Christ (Philippians 3 v 20-21; Romans 8 v 29; 1 John 3 v 2). However we struggle at present to put it all together, God will faithfully close the gap when we are glorified.

Will we have "blood on our hands" if we don't tell people the gospel, and then they die and go to hell?

In Acts 20 Paul makes this statement: "Therefore I declare to you today that I am innocent of the blood of any of you. For I have not hesitated to proclaim to you the whole will of God"(v 26-27). Some take this to mean that we will be held responsible by Jesus for those we have failed to share the gospel with.

We all have the responsibility to tell people about Jesus (Matthew 28 v 18-20; Colossians 4 v 5-6). And God gives us opportunities to do so. Sharing the gospel, like any other command from God, is something that we are going to give an account for. However, to say that we are responsible if we fail to tell people and they die, seems to be an extra step that the Bible does not explicitly take for Christians. In Acts 20 Paul is expressing publicly his faithfulness to the ministry that God has given him. So the emphasis is more on him discharging his duty to share the gospel, rather than his guilt at failing to share it with anyone in particular.

How can three hours on the cross equate with suffering in eternal hell?

We need to think in terms of quality instead of simply quantity. In other words, it is not the length of Christ's suffering but the value of his sacrifice that is the key. Jesus is the perfect Son of God who has infinite value. When he offered himself upon the cross, he was not only able to bear the infinite wrath of God, but also to satisfy it. The eternal Son of God offered an eternal sacrifice to pay our eternal debt and give eternal life. When we think of the price of sin and the value of Christ's sacrifice, we can understand how he fully satisfied God's requirement for our forgiveness.

Is C.S. Lewis right about hell?

One of the most influential writers on Christianity in the 20th century was an Oxford English professor who experienced a remarkable conversion from atheism: C.S. Lewis. He is perhaps best known for his books for children, *The Chronicles of Narnia*, but he also wrote profound and influential books like *Mere Christianity,* in which he deploys his masterful understanding of language and ideas to make perceptive and powerful points.

Lewis looked squarely at the questions of heaven and hell in the last of the Narnia books, *The Last Battle*, but spelled these ideas out in a fascinating work of imaginative fiction called *The Great Divorce*. It is a remarkable and fascinating story that recounts a day trip from hell to heaven by a diverse group of people in a London bus. It is packed with powerful images and fascinating insights. He imagines hell to be a grey and nondescript rainy slum where people can't bear to live close to each other, and so are endlessly moving further and further away from each other. When the "tourists" arrive in heaven, they do not understand it and hate being there, longing to be back "home" in the other place. Brilliantly, Lewis depicts hell, not as a place of equal or greater size to heaven, but as a small crack in the ground, into which the travellers must shrink to return there.

The book and Lewis's ideas in this area have the effect of toning down the difficulties we have about judgement and hell. He presents a hell that is not torment, but just sad and dreary. He presents its inhabitants as continuing in their mindset of rejecting God, rather than being suddenly aware of the truth about God and the gospel, and being appalled at their stupidity in rejecting him. He describes hell as being a place, not where God sends people, but where people voluntarily choose to go. More controversially, he suggests that God is willing, in his grace, to accept the devotion of some people to other "gods" as worship of himself.

Despite the illuminating and intriguing ideas in the book, it is clear that Lewis has searched literature and philosophy for answers to these difficulties, rather than the Scriptures and the teaching of Christ.

Lewis is always worth reading—but the powerful and poetic way he presents his ideas can sometimes blind us to the fact that he may be, and sometimes is, just plain wrong.

How can I answer those who say they will be happy in hell, because that is where their friends are?

This throwaway line is regularly used in conversation, as well as the portrayal of heaven or the new creation as something pallid and utterly boring. Both ideas betray a total misunderstanding of what is at stake.

God is the source of *everything* that is good. Even though we may not acknowledge him as the source of beauty and goodness, everyone daily experiences a thousand blessings from his hands. Love and family; food and wealth; music and the beauty of creation; the gifts and abilities we have; joy and laughter—they are all gifts from God. We enjoy just a part of them now, imperfectly and tainted by the realities of pain and suffering in our fallen world. But for those who have been rescued by Jesus, we will experience that joy in full in the new creation. Perfect friendships, complete joy and love.

But hell will be the absence of all those things. It will involve all the worst things about life here, multiplied many times over, but with no joy, no hope, no love.

"I'll enjoy hell because all my friends will be there."

"No you won't. You won't have any friends in hell—because there will be no friendship there."

What should Christians do in response to the reality of hell?

Certainly, the biblical teaching about hell provides a substantial warning to those who are not yet believers in Jesus. But it is also important for Christians to apply what the Bible says about hell and the realities of the coming judgment. Here are four areas in particular:

- **Gratitude.** Apart from Christ, we deserve to be in hell. Let that sink in for a moment. Our first reaction as those who have responded to the gospel should be a tremendous sense of gratitude to God for his mercy and grace. Instead of giving us what we deserve (eternal punishment), God gives those who have faith in Christ what *he* deserves (eternal blessings).

- **Holiness.** Knowing where sin leads and what sin costs compels Christians to pursue holiness. We should hate sin in ourselves and in others because, at its core, sin is rebellion against God. Having been spared divine wrath, we must pursue Christ-like-ness, which is holiness.

- **Sobriety.** We live in a time when it is fashionable to trivialize nearly everything. Our cultural reflex is to avoid or minimize things that are unsettling. It is inconsistent to respond to the doctrine of hell without sobriety. The Scriptures call us to be sober-minded (1 Peter 1 v 13). We must think clearly about things and feel the gravity of the matter. This does not mean we are joyless or have no fun, but it does mean we are people of substance, who can talk about these matters with the seriousness that they deserve.

- **Evangelism.** If we believe what the Bible says about hell, then we must tell others. There is no other option for anyone. Paul asks how people will hear without a preacher (Romans 10 v 14). The gravity of hell should provoke in us a zeal for compassionate but faithful evangelism.

Acknowledgements

Any project requires many people working together—often unseen—to produce a finished product. I am grateful for the kind and gracious folks at The Good Book Company for the opportunity to work with them on this book. In particular, I am thankful for Tim Thornborough's thoughtful editorial contributions and persistent encouragement.

Most of the questions and a number of the sections in this book came from conversations I had with church members at Emmaus Bible Church in Omaha—a congregation which I am blessed to pastor. I am thankful for the many interactions on this topic and the thoughtful feedback after the sermons and question and answer session that followed them. Thomas Anderson was a great help in providing initial editorial help and review.

Finally, I am thankful to my family—and especially to my wife, Christie—for their sacrifice of time, and their valuable feedback and unrelenting encouragement. Your support means more than you could ever imagine.

※

I am grateful to Edward Donnelly for the illustration about a cancer doctor that I used on page 12. http://www.sermonaudio.com/sermoninfo.asp?SID=62608204465

I am also grateful for Gregg Allison's explanation of the three strands of alternative Christian teaching on hell (page 24): Gregg R. Allison, *Historical Theology* (Zondervan, 2011), p 702.

BIBLICAL | RELEVANT | ACCESSIBLE

At The Good Book Company, we are dedicated to helping Christians and local churches grow. We believe that God's growth process always starts with hearing clearly what he has said to us through his timeless word—the Bible.

Ever since we opened our doors in 1991, we have been striving to produce resources that honor God in the way the Bible is used. We have grown to become an international provider of user-friendly resources to the Christian community, with believers of all backgrounds and denominations using our Bible studies, books, evangelistic resources, DVD-based courses and training events.

We want to equip ordinary Christians to live for Christ day by day, and churches to grow in their knowledge of God, their love for one another, and the effectiveness of their outreach.

Call us for a discussion of your needs or visit one of our local websites for more information on the resources and services we provide.

Your friends at The Good Book Company

NORTH AMERICA	thegoodbook.com	866 244 2165
UK & EUROPE	thegoodbook.co.uk	0333 123 0880
AUSTRALIA	thegoodbook.com.au	(02) 9564 3555
NEW ZEALAND	thegoodbook.co.nz	(+64) 3 343 2463

 WWW.CHRISTIANITYEXPLORED.ORG
Our partner site is a great place for those exploring the Christian faith, with a clear explanation of the good news, powerful testimonies and answers to difficult questions.

ISBN 978-1-78498-068-9

9 781784 980689

thegoodbook.com | co.uk   Christian Theology / Systematic